Lockheed Constellation in colour

SCOTT HENDERSON

SCOVAL
PUBLISHING LTD

© 2005 Scott Henderson
Written By Scott Henderson

British Library Cataloguing in Publication Data
A catalogue record for this book is available from the British Library

ISBN: 1 902236 12 2

Published by:
SCOVAL Publishing Ltd.
PO BOX 36
Ponteland
Newcastle-upon-Tyne
NE20 9WE
England
Tel: (01661) 820 838
Fax: (01661) 822 911
Email: scovalpublishing@tiscali.co.uk

Printed by Kyodo Printing Co (S'Pore) Pte Ltd.
Singapore

Edited by C Hymers and Roy James
Produced and typeset in 11pt on 14pt Quorum
Designed by Scott Henderson, for SCOVAL Publishing Ltd.

ACKNOWLEDGEMENTS

The Author and Publisher wish to thank the following companies and individuals for their kind help in the preparation of this book :—

Eric Schulzinger and Denny Lombard (Lockheed Martin Aeronautics Company), Robert D Archer, Leon Franco, Peter R Keating (sadly deceased), J Hunt, Mel Lawrence, Lufthansa, Pierre-Alain Petit, N Raith, Charles T Robbins, Brian Stainer, Henry Tenby ("http://www.AirlineHobby.com"), Scotpic, Nikky Scherrer, Lawrence Smalley, Harry Sievers, Tom Singfield, Dean Slaybaugh and TAHS.

Every effort has been made to identify the source of illustrations in this publication but this has not been possible in all cases. The Publisher and Author wish to apologise to anyone who has not been acknowledged.

PREFACE

As far as I aware this is the first time that a colour profile on the Lockheed Constellation has been produced. Wherever possible I have tried to provide unseen photographs of the aircraft from many sources, but unfortunately have been unable to find a sample of all liveries and types in colour. Nevertheless I hope that you enjoy this latest publication from Scoval Publishing.

Scott Henderson, Ponteland
January 2005

CONTENTS

INTRODUCTION

The credit for the introduction into service of arguably the most aesthetically beautiful piston-engined airliner ever designed, can be laid at the door of Howard Hughes, the famous playboy, record breaking pilot, film producer and industrialist. It was on behalf of his airline, Transcontinental & Western Air, later to become Trans World Airlines, that he decided to approach US airframe manufacturers in 1939, with the request for a new design of airliner that would be able to fly coast to coast non-stop in the USA, at a speed of around three hundred miles per hour with a maximum range of 3,500 miles.

At the time of this approach, the twin-engined Douglas DC3 sleeper transports had been in service for a mere three years, and even though it could fly coast to coast, it took a maximum of 17-18hrs and at least three stops to achieve this. Lockheed decided to submit a proposal to build a four-engined aircraft of elegant design, to be called the Constellation, and this was accepted by Hughes. Hughes then negotiated a tough contract with Lockheed which prevented the manufacturer from selling the aircraft to any other airline for a period of two years after entry of service.

The prototype was completed under the leadership of designer C L Kelly Johnson by the end of 1942, by adapting a current design he was working on called the Excalibur, developing it into the L-049 Excalibur. It was renamed the Constellation and the first flight took place on 9th January 1943. Unfortunately the airlines, which by this time were beating a path to Lockheed's door, discovered that the US Army Air Force had decided to incorporate all Constellation production into military service for the duration of the Second World War.

The prototype Constellation registered NX25600 originally ordered by TWA was taken over by the US Army and painted in olive drab camouflage and designated C-69-1-LO. It made its maiden flight on 9th January 1943 from the Lockheed Air Terminal at Burbank, California.

After hostilities had ended, Lockheed developed the Constellation through series L-649 and L-749, providing improved performance and accommodation and on development of turbo-compound engines,

faster speed and efficiency in the form of the L-1049 Super Constellation and finally, on to the ultimate propliner, the L-1649 Starliner.

The Connie was also adopted by both the US Navy and Air Force in large numbers and used for Airborne Early Warning radar, electronic, atmospheric research and weather reconnaissance, maritime reconnaissance, airborne TV and Radio transmitter station, engine test beds, general transport of troops and supplies, and many other unusual and special duties including support for the Blue Angels display team.

The Super Constellation was also operated by the French, Indian and Indonesian Air Forces and also the Indian Navy.

The total number of Constellations built was as follows:-

L-C69/L-049 Constellations = 88

L-649/L-749 Constellations = 145

L-1049 Super Constellation = 579

L-1649A Starliner = 44

A grand total of 856 aircraft were delivered.

At the time this book was being written, the Constellation was making a comeback within the preservation movement. Two aircraft were actively flying in the US, a L-1049H Super Constellation based at Kansas City in full TWA colours, and C-121A in full MATS colours based at Avra Valley, Arizona. There are also two more flying in Europe; ex-C-121C Super Constellation (N7354) based at Basil in Switzerland, and the Netherlands ex-C121A (N749VR) restored to full KLM early livery based at the Dutch Aviodrome Museum. Last but not least Australia's Historical Aviation Restoration Society fly their beautiful ex-C-121C in full Qantas colours on the Australian airshow circuit. There are also a number of Constellations which are in potential airworthy condition including two Starliners so who knows what the future may bring.

LOCKHEED XC69/L-049 CONSTELLATION

C/N1961-XC69
In company with a Lockheed Vega, the prototype Constellation is prepared for flight by Lockheed engineers prior to the maiden flight of the aircraft which took place on 9th January 1943, from the Lockheed Air Terminal at Burbank, California, and flown to the Muroc Army Air Base in the Mojave Desert where it made four local flights and then returned to Burbank on the same day. The aircraft was inspected, modified and had nose and main wheel doors fitted in readiness for its seventh flight which took place on 18th January 1943.
Scott Henderson Collection

C/N 1967
After twelve years service with El Al, 4X-AKB is seen here at Heathrow Airport in February 1962 whilst taking a break during the delivery flight to Universal Sky Tours. The company purchased the aircraft to be operated by Euravia (London)Ltd., for inclusive tour flights to European Mediterranean destinations. The aircraft was withdrawn from use and scrapped at Luton in May 1965.
Peter R Keating - Scott Henderson Collection

LOCKHEED L-049 CONSTELLATION

C/N 1969
Originally delivered to the USAF in March 1945 before being bought by TWA, and then serving with the airline for over twelve years as N90830, this aircraft was then purchased by Aero Transport on 26th June 1961 and registered OE-IFA for use on the long-haul IT market. The first Intercontinental flight was made on 18th August 1961, followed by flights to Singapore, Nairobi and Tokyo. Unfortunately financial problems led to Aero Transport having to cease flying in October 1963 and to be declared bankrupt in February 1964. Withdrawn from use and stored at Vienna-Schwechat Airport, Austria the Connie was finally broken up in June 1966.
Peter R Keating

C/N 1970
N90831 "Star of Switzerland" was originally delivered to Transcontinental & Western Air on 17th May 1950 after service with the US Air Force, and was the tenth Constellation built and the oldest to survive. Wearing the livery of her first civil owner, TWA, she is seen in retirement at the Pima County Air & Space Museum, Arizona in August 1999 after serving with a total of nine different airlines.
Scott Henderson

LOCKHEED L-049 CONSTELLATION

C/N 1970
N90831 is seen here at Tucson Arizona in September 1970 during service with Lake Havasu City, one of a number of airlines that used the Constellation to transport customers to and from Casinos in the west of the USA.
Dean Slaybaugh

C/N 1976
First serving with the British Overseas Airways Corporation as G-AHEK "Berwick", N2737A of Imperial Airways is seen at Gatwick Airport, England in July 1961. The aircraft was used in the company of two other L-049s for US Government military charter flights. During one of these flights on 8th November 1961, a mere five months after this photograph was taken, the aircraft was lost in a crash near Richmond Virginia in which all 74 passengers and three of the five crew were killed.
Peter R Keating

LOCKHEED L-049 CONSTELLATION

C/N 1977

Trans European Airways bought G-AHEL, also a former British Overseas Airways Corporation aircraft, from Falcon Airways in July 1961. Here the aircraft sits idle on a fine sunny day at Gatwick Airport one month later in August 1961. After being withdrawn from use and stored temporarily at Luton Bedfordshire in October 1962, the aircraft was sold to Euravia (London) Ltd. on 23rd June 1963 and introduced into service operating inclusive tour flights for Universal Sky Tours.
Peter R Keating

C/N 1977

Euravia (London) Ltd. sold G-AHEL to Britair East Africa Ltd. in November 1964 who re-registered it as 5Y-ABF and made it their flagship. The aircraft was repainted and delivered to the company at its European base at Rotterdam on 19th December 1964, with the intention of using it on tourist charter flights to Nairobi and Mombassa. In the autumn of 1965 Britair ceased all operations, at which point 5Y-ABF was ferried to Shannon where the aircraft was finally broken up in 1968.
Brian Stainer

LOCKHEED L-049 CONSTELLATION

C/N 2023
*Delivered new to TWA (Transcontinental & Western Air) on 20th December 1945 and named "Star of the Pyramids",
N86502 prepares for departure at an unidentified airport where she shares the ramp
with a company DC-3, sometime in 1947.*
Scott Henderson Collection

C/N 2027
*In November 1965 at Mexico City Airport, N86506 wears the colourful livery of Aerospace Traveler, a US based travel
club, prior to her return flight to the USA.*
Dean Slaybaugh

LOCKHEED L-049 CONSTELLATION

C/N 2038
Originally delivered to Pan American Airways as "Clipper Donald McKay" on 21st January 1946. After conversion to Series L-149, N88838 was sold to Panair do Brasil on 7th December 1953. Here the aircraft shares the ramp with three other company Constellations at Aeroporto Santos Dumont, Rio de Janeiro, in June 1962.
Scott Henderson

C/N 2051
G-AMUP was another former British Overseas Airways Corporation aircraft. She was bought from Capital Airlines of the USA in December 1960, along with two others, by Captain Marian Kozubski, Managing Director and Chief Pilot of Falcon Airways. Unfortunately due to problems with the airworthiness authorities in the UK, the airline was destined to operate the aircraft for only six months before being grounded after the company ceased trading. Here we see G-AMUP at Heathrow Airport on 5th June 1961.
Note the Skyways York in the background.
Peter R Keating

LOCKHEED L-049 CONSTELLATION

C/N2052
Ex-American Overseas Airways' L-049, N90922 became XA-MAG in February 1957 under lease from Pan American
Airways, joining another L-049 Constellation for a few months of internal service in Mexico during that year.
The airline did purchase its own L-0749 in early 1958 but all the Connies were replaced with the
Bristol Britannia when it entered service with the airline in late 1958-1959.
Scott Henderson Collection

C/N2053
Delivered as "Flagship Great Britain" to American Overseas Airlines in March 1946 and destined to fly with Pan
American and also Delta Airlines, N90923, one of four 049 Constellations used by
American Flyers, sits in the sunshine looking immaculate at
Memphis, Tennessee in November 1965.
Mel Lawrence

LOCKHEED L-049 CONSTELLATION

C/N 2059
On 6th December 1965 at Rio de Janeiro, PP-PDQ "Jeronimo Fragoso de Albuquerque" prepares for
another flight in the service of Panair do Brasil. The aircraft served with the airline
for a total of twelve years before being broken up in her native Brazil in 1969.
Scott Henderson Collection

C/N 2064
Originally delivered to American Overseas Airlines in March 1946 as "Flagship Eire", N90926 became Pan American
"Clipper Ocean Herald" when the two airlines merged in September 1950. The aircraft was destined to serve
the airline for a mere two years before onward sale to Trans World Airlines as "Star of Tunis".
Peter R Keating

LOCKHEED L-049 CONSTELLATION

C/N2068
One of five L-049 Constellations operated by Modern Air Transport on freight and ad-hoc passenger charters beginning in August 1962, N86531 sits on the Denver ramp in rather unseasonable weather in June 1965.
Mel Lawrence

C/N2070
Built for Royal Dutch Airlines and delivered to the airline in June 1946 as PH-TAW, here we see the aircraft in the guise of N6000C after service with twelve previous owners, still looking in excellent condition at an unknown airfield in the USA on 18th April 1971, just one month after the aircraft was bought by Full Gospel Native Missionary.
Dean Slaybaugh

LOCKHEED L-049 CONSTELLATION

C/N2071
Capital Airlines based in Washington DC was one of most successful US domestic airlines during the 1950s. They operated a total of twelve L-049 Constellations which unusually contained a forward "Cloud Club" lounge seating eight people with the main cabin accommodating 56. Here we see N86533 disembarking passengers at Miami in July 1959. After service with Capital Airlines, the aircraft went on to serve with Rymar and was leased to The International Caribbean Corporation in August 1965. During a visit to Paraguay on 8th September 1965, the aircraft was seized by the authorities for smuggling and is believed to survive to this day at Asuncion, albeit in a run-down state.
Mel Lawrence - Scott Henderson Collection

C/N2072
This aircraft was delivered new to Air France as F-BAZA in September 1946, and then sold in 1950 to TWA who named her "Star of the Azores" and operated the aircraft until August 1959 when they sold her to California Airmotive who also sold it on. Thereafter it was operated by many small operators until June 1968, when bought by Mineral County Airlines and operated as Hawthorne Nevada Airlines on the Casino route from Los Angeles to Hawthorne in 1968. She is seen here at an unidentified airfield in April 1969.
Scott Henderson Collection

LOCKHEED L-049 CONSTELLATION

C/N2075
N9414H flew for Air France, Trans World Airlines and Eastern Airlines, before finding its way to Paradise Airlines
under a period of lease during 1964 from the then owner, Nevada Airmotive. Here the aircraft
takes time-off services at Oakland California during that year.
Mel Lawrence

C/N2078
The airline most identified with the Lockheed Constellation is Trans World Airlines. Here N90816 is serviced at San
Francisco Airport in August 1959, surrounded by an interesting selection of propliners and an early TWA 707.
The aircraft was sold to Nevada Airmotive in March 1962.
Mel Lawrence - Scott Henderson Collection

LOCKHEED L-049 CONSTELLATION

C/N2078
Taken at Phoenix in September 1970, N90816 was one of two Constellations owned by Pacific Air Transport based at Santa Rosa. She was used on charter services until withdrawn from service in 1970 and then lingered on at Fort Lauderdale, Florida until being broken up in the 1980s.
Dean Slaybaugh

C/N2085
Aerovias Nacionales Quisqueyana operated six Constellations during twelve years of scheduled flights within the Caribbean, starting in 1966 until the suspension of passenger carrying flights following a ban by the Dominican authorities in 1978. Here we see HI-270 in happier times in March 1978 prior to the cessation of flying. Trado bought the aircraft in 1970 and it was broken up for spares in July 1980.
Scott Henderson Collection

LOCKHEED L-749 CONSTELLATION

C/N2504
G-ANTF was Ace Freighter's first L-749 Constellation and a former Air India, Qantas, BOAC and Transocean Airlines aircraft. She is seen here at Gatwick on 19th May 1965 wearing the company's second livery. At Aden in March 1966 the aircraft was damaged in a landing accident but was repaired and returned to service. She was withdrawn from use at Coventry in September 1966 and scrapped there in 1971.
Peter R Keating

C/N2522
Quisqueyana became famous for operating the last scheduled passenger carrying Constellation flight. At Miami in April 1976, HI-207 "Duarte" is prepared to receive passengers for the short flight to the Dominican Republic.
The aircraft is still believed to exist, although derelict, at Agua Jira, Columbia.
Scott Henderson Collection

LOCKHEED L-649/749 CONSTELLATION

C/N2523
Delivered new to the airline on 5th June 1947, N106A carrying the striking "Fly-Eastern" early colour scheme in 1959, taxies to the runway closely pursued by a United Airlines DC-7.
Mel Lawrence

C/N2534
LANSA (Lineas Aereas Nacionales S.A.) decided to introduce the forward thinking idea of introducing low-fare services in Peru in 1964 with four L-749 Constellations. This aircraft was purchased in March 1964, initially registered as OB-WAC-740 and later that year re-registered as OB-R-740 and named "Ciudad de Tacna". The aircraft was finally withdrawn from service at Lima in 1974 and later broken up in 1981.
Pierre-Alain Petit - Scott Henderson Collection

LOCKHEED L-649/749 CONSTELLATION

C/N2538
Bought by the Government of Senegal from Air France, registered 6V-AAR and named "Fleche des Almadies" in March
1966, this Constellation was used as a VIP aircraft for just over five years until finally withdrawn and
stored at Toussus-le-Noble near Paris France, where she was eventually broken up in July 1979.
Dean Slaybaugh

C/N2540
Originally delivered to KLM Royal Dutch Airlines in August 1947 as PH-TEP and named "Pontianak", until being
re-registered as PH-LDR in 1954, this Connie is seen here in this rare photograph wearing
classic natural metal livery, while boarding passengers at an unidentified airport.
Henry Tenby (AirlineHobby.com)

LOCKHEED L-649/749 CONSTELLATION

C/N2540

Aerotransport Entre Rios was formed in 1962 as a specialist non-scheduled freight carrier transporting horses and cattle. The airline operated this single model L-749 from April 1964 for three years and then put her into storage. She was brought back into service for a futher 18 months in July 1970 after the company Britannia crashed. At Mexico City on the 16th April 1966, LV-IGS sits idle on the rainsoaked ramp.
Scott Henderson Collection via Henry Tenby

C/N2547

Delivered new to Air France on 10th September 1947, F-BAZO was destined to spend nearly thirteen years flying for the airline before being transferred in June 1961 to the Government SGACC and operated by the French Air Force for search and rescue duties. On a sunny day at Paris-Orly in June 1959, F-BAZO shares the ramp with a Royal Air Maroc L-749A Connie and an Air France Caravelle, while being prepared for another scheduled flight.
Scott Henderson

LOCKHEED L-649/749 CONSTELLATION

C/N2547
A rare shot taken during the two month lease to Tunis Air from Air France in June 1961, F-BAZO wears the full colours of the airline during servicing for the return flight to Tunis from Paris-Orly. Note the speedpak under the fuselage in the loading position.
Scott Henderson Collection

C/N2549
A superb shot of BOAC's G-ALAL "Banbury", surrounded by a fascinating selection of ground equipment, taken at Hong Kong in June 1956, exactly eight years after delivery to the airline.
Peter R Keating

LOCKHEED L-649/749 CONSTELLATION

C/N2549
*Euravia's G-ALAL on final approach to Zurich in September 1964. Note the oil stained engine nacelles and flaps,
demonstrating the extensive use of the Constellation by Euravia.
via Nikky Scherrer*

C/N2549
*An atmospheric shot of Euravia's G-ALAL taken at Luton Airport in January 1964, in the company of a European
Airways and a Skyways Constellation. The aircraft served with Aerlinte Eireann Irish Airlines and BOAC as
"Banbury" and Skyways of London, before being purchased by Euravia (London) Ltd. in September 1962
who operated the aircraft until February 1965 when it was sold to Ace Freighters.
Peter R Keating*

LOCKHEED L-649/749 CONSTELLATION

C/N2549
COPISA of Peru operated OB-R-899 on cargo routes from Peru to various South American
destinations and Miami, Florida in the USA.
Scott Henderson Collection

C/N2551
From December 1959, Koreanair (Korean National Airlines) operated Constellation L-749A (HL102) to various
destinations in the Far East for a total of two years and three months, before sale to Aer Transport of
Austria. HL102 is serviced on the ramp at Kai Tak Airport, Hong Kong
in the company of a Civil Air Transport DC-6B.
Peter R Keating

LOCKHEED L-649/749 CONSTELLATION

C/N2553
*Currently preserved at the Science Museum, Wroughton, England in spurious TWA markings after flying for UK carrier
Lanzair (Channel Islands) Ltd., N7777G displays the livery of Wein Alaska Airlines "Arctic Liner Arlis" while
in service hauling freight at Fairbanks in June 1968. Note the aircraft is fitted with a speedpak.*
Scott Henderson Collection

C/N2555
*Previously flying with Eastern Airlines, Aerlinte Eireann Irish Airlines and BOAC as G-ALAN "Beaufort", this aircraft
was purchased from BOAC's stored Constellation fleet at London's Heathrow Airport in March 1959 by Pacific
Northern Airlines, for service as N1554V in the north east of the USA, based at Seattle. On 14th June 1960,
however, N1554V was lost when the aircraft crashed into Mount Gilbert in Alaska, with the loss
of fourteen lives. She is seen here turning onto the stand at Seattle in September 1959.*
Harry Sievers via Peter R Keating

LOCKHEED L-649/749 CONSTELLATION

C/N2556
After the merger between Pacific Northern and Western Airlines in July 1967, N1593V was introduced into the Western fleet, based at Los Angeles, and flew various routes to several Alaskan towns. The airline flew the last US Constellation passenger service in November 1968.
Harry Sievers via Peter R Keating

C/N2557
Avianca Columbia used HK-651 fitted with 80 tourist seats mainly on domestic scheduled services for eight years from May 1959. On a sunny day at Miami in 1960 HK-651, surrounded by support equipment and equipped with a speedpak, is serviced prior to the return flight to Columbia.
Scott Henderson Collection

LOCKHEED L-649/749 CONSTELLATION

C/N2559

Based at Oakland California, Transocean owned four L-749 Constellations and used them mostly for low fare services from California to Hawaii. After increasing competition from jet powered competitors on the airline's most important routes, Transocean found itself unable to raise the funds to purchase comparable aircraft and were forced into bankruptcy in July 1960. N9812F embarks passengers in May 1959 at San Francisco International Airport.
Mel Lawrence - Scott Henderson Collection

C/N2559

Miami Airlines had four L-749A Constellations leased from Babb Co. during 1960, mostly used for passenger charters. One of these, N9812F "Mary H", is seen at London's Heathrow Airport in June 1960 during a brief two month sub-lease to Loftleidir Airlines of Iceland.
Brian Stainer - Scott Henderson Collection

LOCKHEED L-649/749 CONSTELLATION

C/N2562
*Delivered new to Qantas Empire Airways as VH-EAB in October 1947 and after a period of service for BOAC as
G-ANUP "Basildon", this Connie entered service with Skyways of London Ltd. on lease from BOAC in
July 1959. She joined three other L-749s in service with the airline, and was used mostly
for freight as is demonstrated in this shot taken with the rear cargo door open.
Scott Henderson*

C/N2565
*Delivered to Qantas in 1947, EH-EAB "Lawrence Hargrave" is captured in flight in all her glory by the Lockheed
photographer prior to delivery to the airline in October 1947. She was converted to an L-749A and became
G-ANUR "Basildon" serving with BOAC for over four years until July 1959.
Lockheed*

LOCKHEED L-649/749 CONSTELLATION

C/N2565

Aerolineas Uruguayas purchased CX-BHC in January 1968 for non-scheduled cargo flights between Uruguay and Miami, where this shot was taken in June 1968. However the airline only managed a few services before the aircraft was grounded at Montevideo where the L-749A was eventually broken up in 1970.
Scott Henderson Collection

C/N2572

Taken at Singapore, VH-EAC embarks passengers for the next stage of the journey to London. This aircraft was delivered new to Qantas as "Harry Hawker" in October 1947, but after exactly eight years flying for the airline, "Harry" was sold to Aerovias Guest SA in October 1955. The aircraft was broken up for spares at Fox Field, California in 1971.
Peter R Keating - Scott Henderson Collection

LOCKHEED L-649/749 CONSTELLATION

C/N2583
Pictured in flight wearing TWA colours and Lockheed Constellation titles, NC91207 a Series L-749 was destined to serve Trans World Airlines as "Star of Missourri" and later "Star of Milan" for a grand total of eighteen years six months before withdrawal and storage at Kansas City in December 1966. She was eventually broken up there in June 1968.
Lockheed

C/N2601
N494TW served the USAF as a C121A from delivery in December 1948 then, following retirement in 1968, was converted to aerial sprayer configuration. In 1979, she was sold to Beaver Air Spray and registered C-GXKO and later sold on to Conifair Aviation Inc and based at Quebec, Canada. The aircraft was briefly owned by the movie actor John Travolta before being purchased by Vern Raburn and restored into the colours of the "Military Air Transport Service". She is now world famous as the "MATS Connie" serving on the airshow circuit worldwide. Here we see N494TW at Tucson, Ryan Field in November 1987, in storage while still in the ownership of John Travolta. In late 2004 the aircraft was sold in Korea to be used on the airshow circuit in the Far East wearing the colours of Korean Air.
Charles T Robbins

LOCKHEED L-649/749 CONSTELLATION

C/N2601
The "MATS Connie" is seen taking off during the tour of Europe undertaken by the aircraft in the summer months of 1998. Note the superb highly polished finish of the aircraft.
Scott Henderson

C/N2606
Here we see "Columbine 1" (48-614), the personal aircraft of General Dwight Eisenhower, which was named after the state flower of Lady Eisenhower's home state of Colorado and is currently preserved at Pima County Air Museum. Being one of ten C121A aircraft ordered by the USAF, she was designed for heavy cargo and passenger transport, able to carry 44 passengers or twenty stretchers and medical attendants. She is photographed taxiing to the runway at an unidentified location in France in the 1960s.
Scott Henderson Collection

LOCKHEED L-649/749 CONSTELLATION

C/N2606
*On a sunny day at London's Heathrow Airport the ex "Columbine 1", now carrying the serial 0-80614
and wearing the final colours carried in service, sits idle prior to being withdrawn from service
and storage at Davis Monthan Air Force Base in October 1966.*
Scott Henderson Collection

C/N2610
*Rutas Internacionales Peruanas S.A. used one L-749A to fly cargo between Lima and Miami, from September
1966 until it was withdrawn from use in May 1968.*
TAHS

LOCKHEED L-649/749 CONSTELLATION

C/N2611

Whilst in the service of the Federal Aviation Administration, N116A crashed during a training flight at Topham Field, Canton Island in the Pacific, caused by the reversal of No. 4 prop during circuits and bumps. Here we see the aircraft in happier times wearing the colours of Eastern Airlines at La Guardia in the late 1950's.
Robert D Archer

C/N2614

An unusual view of ex-Eastern Airlines L-749A as it taxies at Miami on 17th December 1963 carrying the duel registrations of N117A and OB-WAA. The aircraft was eventually named "Ciudad de Cuzco" and served with Lineas Aéreas Nacionales S.A. (LANSA) for three years until she was broken up at Lima, Peru in 1968.
Dean Slaybaugh

LOCKHEED L-649/749 CONSTELLATION

C/N2620
First serving with Air India as VT-DAS "Himalayan Princess", N5595A of International Aircraft Services was damaged beyond repair when she was involved in a ground collision with a Douglas DC-7 at Oakland Airport on 20th June 1961. Here she is photographed one month before the accident at Oakland.
Lawrence Smalley - Scott Henderson Collection

C/N2620
This shot was taken shortly after the accident and demonstrates the extent of the damage suffered by N5595A in the collision on the 20th June 1961.
Lawrence Smalley - Scott Henderson Collection

LOCKHEED L-649/749 CONSTELLATION

C/N2621
PH-LDN "Vlaardingen" is seen at London Heathrow in preparation for the return trip to Amsterdam on 12th August 1958. The aircraft was destined to spend its whole life flying for KLM until being withdrawn from use at Schipol Airport, Amsterdam and broken up there in 1962.
Scott Henderson Collection

C/N2623
Flying over the west coast of the USA prior to delivery to South African Airways as "Capetown", ZS-DBR displays the first colours to good affect. After delivery to the aircraft's second owner, Ace Freighters as G-ASYS in November 1964, the aircraft appears to have languished at Bagington Airport, Coventry until being broken up in April 1967.
Lockheed

LOCKHEED L-649/749 CONSTELLATION

C/N2627
CN-CCP is photographed at London Gatwick in August 1960 sporting the attractive colours of Royal Air Maroc.
This shot was taken approximately half-way through the eighteen months that the aircraft would fly for
this airline, before onward sale to COPISA of Peru.
Scott Henderson Collection

C/N2627
In June 1970 OB-R-898, owned by COPISA but operated by Peru International, takes a brief rest at Mexico City whilst
on the weekly service from Miami to Lima. The aircraft flew as one of five L-749As in the fleet
on mixed passenger-cargo flights until the last aircraft was retired in the late 1970s.
Leon Franco - Henry Tenby - Scott Henderson Collection

LOCKHEED L-649/749 CONSTELLATION

C/N2629
After flying with Air France for ten years, F-BAZT was transferred to Secrétariat Général á L'Aviation Civile et Commerciale (SGACC) in 1960 and modified for search and rescue duties. It was one of seven ex-Air France L-749As based at Toulouse-Francazai operated by the French Air Force for search and rescue missions before being withdrawn from service in December 1969 and broken up in 1971.
Scott Henderson Collection

C/N2630
ZS-DBS "Louis Trichardt", newly painted in Trek Airways livery, was caught on camera by Peter Keating at Johannesburg-Jan Smuts Airport only a matter of days before she started a two-year lease period from South African Airways in November 1961.
Peter R Keating

LOCKHEED L-649/749 CONSTELLATION

C/N2630
G-ASYF of Ace Scotland, a passenger-charter operation formed by Ace Freighters for services from Glasgow-Abbotsinch to Mediterranean destinations, sits out of service at Coventry-Bagington Airport on 15th April 1967. The aircraft was destined to fly the final Constellation flight for Ace Freighters on 14th September 1967 when she flew from Gatwick to Coventry for the last time.
Peter R Keating

C/N2632
ZS-DBU "Durban" delivered to South African Airways in July 1950 was one of four L-0749 Constellations delivered new to the airline, starting from April 1950. They were used on the London-Johannesburg route, carrying a maximum of fifty-three passengers. At London Airport Northside "Durban" carrying later colours sporting a white cabin roof, prepares to return to South Africa.
Bob Archer

LOCKHEED L-649/749 CONSTELLATION

C/N2638

Air Ceylon chartered PH-LDP from KLM Royal Dutch Airlines for 33 months in full colours and named her "Mahadevi" to re-start services from Columbo to London in February 1956. The aircraft was replaced with an L-1049G Super Constellation at the end of 1958 to increase seat availability on the route. Here we see PH-LDP on the ground at Paya Lebar Singapore during the London-Colombo service.
Peter R Keating

C/N2640

This aircraft was originally delivered to KLM as PH-TFD in May 1950, then re-registered PH-LDD in April 1954 and operated until withdrawn from service and stored at Amsterdam in March 1960. Compania Aeronautica Uruguaya S.A. (CAUSA) decided to purchase the Constellation for service in Uruguay in November 1963, and used it for over four years until she was withdrawn from service in 1968.
Scott Henderson Collection

LOCKHEED L-649/749 CONSTELLATION

C/N2642
L-649A Constellation N86521 is serviced at an unidentified US airport wearing the classic colours of Trans World Airlines. The aircraft was broken up at Kansas City in June 1968.
Scott Henderson Collection

C/N2645
Taken at Lima, Peru in June 1967, L-749A (OB-R-917) of Trans Peruana appears to be out of service when in fact she had another two years of flying ahead of her on scheduled passenger services within Peru, in partnership with three other L-749s owned by the airline.
Scott Henderson Collection

LOCKHEED L-649/749 CONSTELLATION

C/N2650

Central American Airways used this L-749A (N273R) in this smart livery for general cargo work based at Louisville Kentucky from October 1967 until she was sold in early 1973. Here we see the aircraft resting at her home base Louisville, in September 1970.
Dean Slaybaugh

C/N2671

Operating over 24 Constellations of various types made Capitol Airways of Nashville, Tennessee the largest non-scheduled operator of the type on the US mainland. N4901C, formerly G-ANNT "Buckingham", was bought from storage at London Heathrow from British Overseas Airways Corporation in March 1958. After the aircraft was withdrawn from service, she was donated to the Bradley Air Museum, Connecticut but unfortunately was destroyed by a tornado on 3rd October 1979. The aircraft is seen here photographed at Wilmington in June 1965 whilst still in service.
Peter R Keating

LOCKHEED L-649/749 CONSTELLATION

C/N2671
A view of the former N4901C, re-registered as N6695C and wearing the rather smart revised colour scheme
of Capitol Airways. This was taken just after donation to the Bradley Air Museum in April 1970.
Scott Henderson Collection

C/N2677
A rare view of F-BBDV, one of two L-749As bought by Air Algerie in January 1956 from Air France for services
to Paris. She was used for a period of six years until withdrawn from use at Maison Blanche Airport
Algiers, Algeria and broken up in 1963.
Scott Henderson Collection

LOCKHEED L-1049 SUPER CONSTELLATION

C/N1961
Bought by Howard Hughes after World War II, the first C-69 (XC-69E) was acquired by Lockheed and stretched to form the Lockheed L-1049 Super Constellation prototype, wearing the registration N67900 and first flying on 13th October 1950, still with the smaller vertical tail and round windows of the earlier marks of Constellation. She was used by Lockheed to test engines and props and also to develop new radar systems until the aircraft was withdrawn from use at Burbank California, and unfortunately broken up in 1959.
Lockheed

C/N4009
Aerotours of Dominicana bought this ex-Eastern Airlines L-1049 in January 1974 and used it for passenger charter flights from Santo Domingo to the Caribbean and South America but from January 1978 it only carried freight. Here the aircraft is seen at Miami preparing for another charter flight south in November 1978.
Scott Henderson

LOCKHEED L-1049 SUPER CONSTELLATION

C/N4011
*Destined to spend its whole service life with Eastern Air Lines, L-1049 (N6211C) is seen at Newark, New Jersey in
January 1962 wearing the special red livery designed for use on the Eastern US passenger "Air-Shuttle Routes".
Eastern Air Lines introduced their 'Air Shuttle' services on 30th April 1961 from New York-Boston and
New York-Washington. The aircraft was withdrawn from use and stored at Opa Locka, Florida,
in February 1968 and eventually scrapped there in 1972.
Mel Lawrence*

C/N4017
*Ex-TWA "Star of the Tiber" on lease/purchase to South Pacific Air Lines (SPAL) of San Francisco operated from
Honolulu to Bora Bora in the Society Islands with connections by local airline Réseau Aérien Interinsulaire
(RAI) using Short Solent flying-boats for the 160 miles to Papéeté Tahiti, then direct Honolulu-Papéeté
flights when Aeroport de Tahiti opened on 16th October 1960. In March 1962 another route
was inaugurated from Honolulu to Pago Pago, in American Samoa, with another ex-TWA
Connie, N6904C leased from June 1962 to January 1964.
SPAL ceased operations in early 1965.
Dean Slaybaugh - Scott Henderson Collection*

LOCKHEED L-1049 SUPER CONSTELLATION

C/N4018
World Wide Airlines of Burbank and Oakland, California leased this ex-TWA Super Constellation "Star of Ganges" from September 1960 for a few months on a military charter contract. It was operated from California to New York, and occasionally charter flights as far afield as Hong Kong, where this photo was taken in September 1960. It also flew for SPAL (see C/N4017).
Scott Henderson Collection

C/N4020
From December 1960, two ex-TWA Lockheed L-1049 Super Constellations were leased by California Hawaiian for services to Hawaii and MATS charters to Europe. Another L-1049 was added to the fleet in 1961 and all three aircraft were used to serve European routes during that year. The airline ceased operating the following year, 1962.
Dean Slaybaugh

LOCKHEED L-1049 SUPER CONSTELLATION

C/N4124
U.S.Navy R7V-1 built in 1953, initially served with VR1 and VR11 Squadrons at Patuxent River. Later as a C-121J, she was operated by the AEW Barrier Squadron at Barbers Point, Hawaii and by Naval Air Technical Training at Memphis. The aircraft was specially modified over the winter of 1967 for the Naval Air Basic Training Command based at Pensicola Florida, with the honour of carrying spares and equipment in support of the US Navy aerobatics team of A4 Skyhawks, The Blue Angels, from March 1968 until being replaced by another Lockheed aircraft, a Hercules, during December 1970.
Mel Lawrence - Scott Henderson Collection

A4 Skyhawks of the United States Navy aerobatic team demonstrate their world famous tight formation aerobatics.
Scott Henderson Collection

LOCKHEED L-1049 SUPER CONSTELLATION

C/N4126

In the company of four Lockheed Neptunes, United States Navy R7V-1 (Bu131625) sits idle wearing rather attractive "Dayglow" colours in June 1962. The aircraft was operated by the early warning Training Unit Atlantic, based at NAS Patuxent River Maryland, from March 1960 to November 1964, when unfortunately the aircraft was written-off in November 1964 during the approach to landing at its base.
Mel Lawrence - Henry Tenby Collection

C/N4132

Two R7V-1s under construction for the U.S. Navy were modified as R7V-2s (Model 1249A-95-75) as engine test-beds, each fitted with four Pratt and Whitney YT34-P-12A Turbo Wasp engines developing 5,550 eshp driving wide chord Hamilton Standard Turbo-Hydromatic three bladed propellers. Two aircraft were modified as YC-121Fs for the U.S. Air Force and the second aircraft is seen here in 1954. It was later modified by Rohr and fitted with Lockheed Model 188 Electra engines for air testing Allison four bladed turboprops.
Lockheed - Henry Tenby (AirlineHobby.com)

LOCKHEED L-1049 SUPER CONSTELLATION

C/N4146
Built for the US Navy as an R7V-1 and delivered in January 1954 as Bu131645, "City of Tachikawa" was operated by
VR-7 and VR-8 Squadrons out of Hickham, Hawaii. Transferred from the Navy to the US Air Force as a C-121G
54-4066 and operated by the Western Transport Air Force (WESTAF) of MATS, she was based with another
30 C-121Gs at Moffet, California and operated to the Pacific, Far East and Australia. The aircraft is
seen in December 1959 at the city of its name, Tachikawa, Japan. It was tragically lost on
12th April 1962 when it crashed at Guam.
Mel Lawrence - Henry Tenby (AirlineHobby.com)

C/N4151
Columbine III, President Eisenhower's personal aircraft, flies over the western US desert. This VC-121E was used as
principal transport from November 1954 until replaced by a VC-137A, a VIP version of the Boeing 707 in 1960. The
aircraft is currently preserved at the USAF Museum at Wright Patterson Air Force Base, Ohio.
Lockheed

LOCKHEED L-1049 SUPER CONSTELLATION

C/N4166
Owned by Seaboard & Western Airlines and delivered to the airline in September 1954, N6504C was one of two Super Constellations leased by British Overseas Airways Corporation for a year from April 1955, for use on daily services from New York to Bermuda and New York to London. In April 1955 at Ildewild, New York, N6504C turns onto its stand wearing the full livery of BOAC.
Harry Sievers via Peter R Keating

C/N4167
This C-121C was acquired by the Australian Historical Aircraft Restoration Society and after restoration in the USA, was re-registered as VH-EAG and flown across the Pacific to Sydney Australia where the aircraft is maintained in flying condition in Qantas colours for display on the airshow circuit.
Bob Shane - Scott Henderson Collection

LOCKHEED L-1049 SUPER CONSTELLATION

C/N4192
Built as a C-121C for the USAF and delivered in February 1956. After a period of storage at Davis Monthan Air Force
Base following retirement from the Air Force, this Connie was bought by DMI Aviation who in turn sold it on to AMSA
(Aerolineas Mondo S.A.) of the Dominican Republic. The aircraft was registered as HI-515CT and named
"City of Santo Domingo", and used on general cargo work from Miami to the Caribbean and South
America until its demise when it crashed into the sea off Puerto Rico on 5th April 1990.
N Raith - Scott Henderson Collection

C/N4320
Delivered to the United States Navy as a WV-2 in January 1955 and operated by Airborne Early Warning Squadrons
VW-2, VW-15 at Patuxent River and VW-4 at Jacksonville, Florida. In 1959 the aircraft was transferred to the
Naval Air Test Centre at Patuxent River for use by their Naval Research Laboratory (NRL) from 1959 to 1976,
and operated as an EC-121N/EC-121P and EC-121K until withdrawal from use in December 1975 to
MASDC at Davis Monthan, Arizona, where it was later scrapped.
Scott Henderson Collection

LOCKHEED L-1049 SUPER CONSTELLATION

C/N4330
In August 1977 at Prestwick Airshow, Scotland, Bu23412, an RC-121D of the 79th AEW & CS of Air Force Reserve (AFRES) based at Homestead AFB, takes time-off from patrolling the North Atlantic whilst supporting NATO against the Soviet threat. The aircraft was retired to Davis Monthan in 1978, where it was eventually scrapped.
Scotpick

C/N4416
Bu141292, a WV-2 built in 1956, was operated by VW-11 and VW-13 at Patuxent River and by June 1962 by the Airborne Early Warning Training Unit. She was modified to an EC-121K and later to an EC-121P and then operated by VAQ-33 Tactical Electronic Warfare Squadron 33, the "Firebirds", who simulated hostile aircraft and transmitted electronic signals for the training of armed forces. She is seen being prepared for another patrol at Tinker Air Force Base in July 1978. This aircraft was destined to fly the last US military Constellation mission in June 1982 and was preserved at Florence Air Museum, South Carolina until she was damaged by fire, whereupon the aircraft was unfortunately scrapped.
Scott Henderson Collection

LOCKHEED L-1049 SUPER CONSTELLATION

C/N4516
Bought by Réné Meyer and used by his airline Compagnie D'Affretments et de Transportes Aériens (Catair), this ex-Air France L-1049C was used from June 1968 for passenger and cargo charters from Paris-Le Bourget and Pontoise to European and Mediterranean destinations until it was sold to Air Fret in October 1973. It was then withdrawn and used for spares at Nimes, until broken up there in 1979. Here we see the aircraft on 19th August 1972 whilst still in active service with Catair.
Scott Henderson Collection

C/N4518
Leased from Air France from June 1967 until return in October 1971 by Réné Meyer, who also owned Air Cameroun, based at Douala Cameroon, West Africa. Meyer used this single L-1049C on internal scheduled freight flights from Douala to Garoua and also passenger and freight charters from Douala to Yaoundé and to Libreville in Gabon. Here we see the aircraft newly delivered to the airline in June 1967.
Scott Henderson Collection

LOCKHEED L-1049 SUPER CONSTELLATION

Ex-Air France Super Constellation F-BGNJ bought by the Spanish airline, Trabajos Aéreos y Enlaces in September 1966 for European inclusive tour services, but was never operated by them for they were unable to gain a licence. EC-BEN is seen at Paris-Orly in June 1967, painted in full colours. The aircraft was eventually sold in September to Air Fret as F-BRAD who operated it from Paris to West Africa until withdrawal in 1973. It was restored into Air France colours for display at the Nantes Museum at Nantes Airport, France.
Scott Henderson Collection

This superb shot of Eastern Air Lines L-1049C (N6225C) was taken just prior to delivery to the airline in January 1954. The aircraft was eventually converted to a freighter with front and rear cargo doors by Lockheed Aircraft Services in May 1960, and scrapped at Fox Field, California in 1971.
Lockheed - Henry Tenby (Airlinehobby.com

LOCKHEED L-1049 SUPER CONSTELLATION

C/N4533
N6225C, one of six Eastern Air Lines all-cargo L-1049Cs stands at New York's JFK Airport in January 1963 wearing Eastern Air Lines attractive "Ship Eastern" livery. The aircraft was sold to California Airmotive Corp. and stored at Fox Field Lancaster until eventually broken-up there in 1972.
Mel Lawrence

C/N4544
L-1049 Super Constellation CF-RNR prepares for another service at Dorval on 19th December 1964 wearing the spectacular colours of World Wide Airways Incorporated of Canada. The aircraft was one of three Model L-1049Gs owned by associate company Montreal Air Services Ltd. The airline stopped flying when its licence was withdrawn on 15th August 1965.
Peter R Keating

LOCKHEED L-1049 SUPER CONSTELLATION

C/N4545
One of six ex-Qantas Super Constellations leased by Twentieth Century Airlines between March 1959 and the fall of the same year, VH-EAH "Southern Sky", now re-registered as N9715C, is seen in March 1960 at Tachi, Japan preparing to start engines for the flight across the Pacific Ocean back to the USA during a "MATS" charter.
Mel Lawrence

C/N4547
VT-DGL "Empress Nurjehan" of Air India International was delivered to the airline in April 1954 and spent eight years in service before being purchased by No. 6 Squadron, Indian Air Force as BG581 in April 1962. The aircraft was then transferred to the Indian Navy in November 1976 and is believed to be stored at Goa in India.
Lockheed

LOCKHEED L-1049 SUPER CONSTELLATION

C/N4551
Delivered new to Iberia as EC-AIO in June 1954 and after conversion to a freighter, this Super Constellation was bought by International Aerodyne in May 1967. She was later sold to Compania Interamericana Export-Import of Panama City in July 1968 and leased to their associate company Rutas Aereas Panamenas S.A. (RAPSA) as HP-475 for charters to the Caribbean and South America. The aircraft was used on cargo flights during the Biafran airlift until withdrawn from use and broken up at Abajan on the Ivory Coast in January 1971.
TAHS

C/N4553
Standing idle at Singapore on 15th March 1959, 4R-ACH "Somadevi" wearing the colourful livery of Air Ceylon is five months into a lease period from KLM Royal Dutch Airlines which began in November 1958. The aircraft was principally used on the Colombo-London route of the airline.
Peter R Keating

LOCKHEED L-1049 SUPER CONSTELLATION

C/N4555

Caught on pushback at JFK Airport, New York in November 1965, HK-176X, was the second of three L-1049Es to be delivered to Aerovias Nacionales de Colombia S.A. (AVIANCA) of Bogata in 1954 and operated to the Caribbean, USA and Europe. This Connie spent fourteen years flying for Avianca after delivery new from Lockheed, until in 1966 the aircraft was transferred to subsidiary Aerotaxi S.A. and operated domestic services until it was withdrawn from service in 1968. She was scrapped at Bogota, Columbia in February 1979.
J Hunt - Scott Henderson Collection

C/N4562

Registered as YV-C-ANF to Linéa Aeropostal Venezolana on 11th November 1954, "Simon Bolivar" taxies at New York JFK airport in July 1959, wearing what must be one of the most attractive liveries ever to grace the Super Constellation.
Mel Lawrence

LOCKHEED L-1049 SUPER CONSTELLATION

C/N4563
American Flyers Airline Inc. who operated four Constellations, bought four Super Constellations in 1964. They expanded domestic services and in 1965 operated transatlantic services to Europe followed, in 1966, by additional services to the Caribbean and Mexico. At Mexico City in July 1966, American Flyers Airline, L-1049C (N9742Z)
sits in the company of sister Constellation N9717C on a charter from the USA.
Leon Franco - Scott Henderson Collection

C/N4565
Taken at Heathrow Airport in October 1968, CF-TGH, one of fourteen Super Constellations used by Trans Canada Air Lines, arrives on stand following another service from North America.
Brian Stainer - Scott Henderson Collection

LOCKHEED L-1049 SUPER CONSTELLATION

C/N4578

In 1959, Capitol Airways Inc. of Nashville operated transatlantic non-military and worldwide MATS charters initially with four L-749As, then adding nine Super Constellations by 1961, and up to eighteen by the mid 1960s, in the process becoming frequent visitors to Europe. Ex-Qantas VH-EAE "Southern Moon" now a L-1049G approaches Gatwick bearing registration N9720C.
Brian Stainer

C/N4579

Qantas operated sixteen Super Constellations on their extensive world network and VH-EAF "Southern Wind" is seen at San Francisco Airport on a cloudy day in August 1959. Qantas operated a round-the-world service so from San Francisco you could fly via Honolulu-Fiji to Sydney or Melbourne or via New York-London to various European and Asian destinations.
Mel Lawrence - Scott Henderson Collection

LOCKHEED L-1049 SUPER CONSTELLATION

C/N4580
*A rare shot of World Wide Airways' owned L-1049E (N9714C) Super Constellation on a visit to London Gatwick in May
1967, whilst on lease from owners International Aerodyne Inc. of Miami to Aerotransport Entre Rios (AER)
of Argentina, who specialised in livestock transport.*
Scott Henderson Collection

C/N4596
*A superb shot of L-1049G (N7115C) "Star of Chilton" of TWA, the largest operator of the Super Constellation.
She was delivered new to the airline in May 1955 and spent all her flying career with TWA
until written-off after a nose wheel collapse at JFK Airport, New York in January 1966.*
Scott Henderson Collection

LOCKHEED L-1049 SUPER CONSTELLATION

C/N4604
Lufthansa had eight Super Constellations which inaugurated their transatlantic scheduled services from Europe to North America on 8th June 1955, to South America in June 1956 and the Middle East from September 1956. Pictured whilst in service at Hanover in April 1962, this Super Connie is now preserved at the Hermeskeil Collection in West Germany. The aircraft flew for over twelve years with Lufthansa before retirement.
Scott Henderson Collection

C/N4607
Trans International operated a fleet of eight Constellations of different marks from Travis AFB, California on both military and freight charters to Hawaii and the Far East from 1960 until its demise in late 1967. Purchased from Lockheed in September 1964, N9751C served the airline until being withdrawn and stored at Oakland, California on 19th September 1964. The aircraft is seen here in June 1968 at an unidentified airport, fifteen months before retirement from service with Trans International.
Scott Henderson Collection

LOCKHEED L-1049 SUPER CONSTELLATION

C/N4614
Ex-Air India VT-DHM "Rani of Ellora", was bought by the Indian Air Force on 30th October 1961 and then eventually transferred to the Indian Navy in November 1976 as IN315. New avionics were fitted to enable the aircraft to operate in maritime reconnaissance and search and rescue missions, replacing Consolidated B-24 Liberators. The Navy Connies were retired in 1984, making them the last Military Constellations in global service.
Scott Henderson Collection

C/N4618
Transportes Aéreos Portugueses' (TAP) third L-1049G, CS-TLC was delivered in September 1955 to replace DC-4s on the Lisbon to Portugese Colony routes to Southern Africa, being Luanda in Angola and Lourenco Marques in Mozambique, and later operated on routes in Europe and some domestic services. Retired in September 1967, the aircraft was used under the false registration of 5T-TAF by International Aerodyne on the Biafran Airlift, during which the aircraft was impounded at Luqa, Malta. She was eventually sold at auction, and was towed one mile from the old RAF airfield of Safi Strip and converted to a restaurant, until she was damaged by arsonists in 1997.
Brian Stainer

LOCKHEED L-1049 SUPER CONSTELLATION

C/N4619
*Looking rather smart whilst on the ramp at Gatwick in the summer of 1966 is Capitol Airways L-1049G
Super Constellation N4903C. The aircraft was bought in January 1960 from Lockheed
and after eight years of flying for Capitol was withdrawn at Wilmington,
Delaware in 1968 and finally broken up there in 1970.*
Peter R Keating

C/N4629
*Flying Dutchman L-1049G (PH-LKE) "Pegasus" flies over the Sierra Nevada mountains on a test flight prior to delivery
to KLM. The aircraft spent its whole life flying for Royal Dutch Airlines before being withdrawn from
use and eventually broken up at Amsterdam in July 1964.*
Lockheed

LOCKHEED L-1049 SUPER CONSTELLATION

C/N4634
In June 1969, F-BHBI sits idle on the Heathrow ramp following a charter flight from Paris. The Super Constellations of Air France, of which fourteen were operated, were occasional visitors to London on the odd scheduled flight from Paris when loads warranted or when the normal scheduled aircraft, usually a Viscount, became unserviceable.
Peter R Keating

C/N4659
Delivered new to Eastern Airlines on 12th October 1956, L-1049G (N6234G) pictured here in August 1967 wears the last blue "Hockey stick" livery which the Super Constellation was to carry whilst in the service of the airline.
Scott Henderson Collection

LOCKHEED L-1049 SUPER CONSTELLATION

C/N4671
Formed in 1964 to provide passenger and freight charter flights from France, Compagnie Air Fret owned four L-1049G's until three were sold in 1969. The company had the distinction of being the last European civil Conny operator when it retired the last aircraft in September 1976. The aircraft was sold to Air Classic and flown to Düsseldorf on 27th June 1978 and put on display. It has now been moved to F.J. Strauss International Airport, Munich and displayed in the colours of Lufthansa as D-ALAP.
via Tom Singfield - Scott Henderson Collection

C/N4672
The first of three L-1049G's sold to Thai Airways International, seen on a test flight from Long Beach, California. Thai found the Constellation to be too complex and experienced difficulties maintaining them, so early in 1958 they were stored at Bangkok. After discussions with Scandinavian Airline Systems (SAS) a new company was formed, Thai Airways International (THAI) with TAC having a 70% shareholding and SAS 30%. Operations began with leased SAS Douglas DC-6Bs, which made the Constellations surplus to requirement, so accordingly they were sold to Guest Aerovias of Mexico, a company which SAS had a major shareholding in.
Lockheed - via Henry Tenby (AirlineHobby.com)

LOCKHEED L-1049 SUPER CONSTELLATION

C/N4673
Displaying the early livery of Iberia Lineas Aereas Españolas, EC-AMP "San Juan" flies over the California coast prior to delivery. The aircraft operated Iberia's transatlantic route network from Spain to New York and South America with European summer flights in the early 1960's for subsidiary Aviaco. Fitted with a freight door in 1964 it continued with the airline until 1967 when sold to International Aerodyne and stored at Miami. The Connie was lost in a crash at La Rioja, approximately 600 miles north west of Buenos Aires, Argentina, and burnt out, probably by the crew who were never found, to disguise the freight being carried. (probably drugs).
Lockheed - via Henry Tenby (AirlineHobby.com)

C/N4675
CU-T-631 was one of three Super Constellations operated by Compañia Cubana de Aviation (CUBANA) on services from Havana, Cuba to New York, Madrid and Mexico City. They were replaced by the Bristol Britannia on the service to Mexico City in December 1958 and to New York in January 1959. When the Cuban Government was taken over by Fidel Castro, the US authorities brought in an embargo with the consequences that the Super Constellations were grounded at Havana for lack of spares and were eventually scrapped.
Lockheed - via Henry Tenby (AirlineHobby.com)

LOCKHEED L-1049 SUPER CONSTELLATION

C/N4676
Delivered new to Iberia and named "Palos de Moguer" in August 1957, EC-AMQ a L-1049G, was converted into a freighter in March 1964 and operated for three more years before being withdrawn from service. She was sold to International Aerodyne in May 1957 and was later broken up at Miami in September 1970.
Scott Henderson Collection

C/N4677
CS-TLE of TAP Transportes Aéreos Portugueses, was leased from Southern Aircraft Holdings Ltd. of Nassau in May 1961 in full colours as "Salvador Correia". The airline used the aircraft for international flights from Lisbon for four years until return to the leaser at Miami in June 1967.
Scott Henderson Collection

LOCKHEED L-1049 SUPER CONSTELLATION

C/N4677
Originally built as the second Super Constellation for the short lived Thai Airways, and registered as HS-TCB in August 1957, the L-1049G passed through a varied list of owners including Guest Aerovias Mexico before finally ending up in the hands of International Aerodyne who purchased the Connie in July 1967. After a period in store at Miami the aircraft was registered N833D and carried this unusual livery for six months until onward sale to Air Cargo Operations in March 1969.
Dean Slaybaugh

C/N4678
Guest Aerovias S.A. purchased XA-NAF from Thai Airways in September 1959 and used the aircraft on services from Mexico City to Miami as well as transatlantic services via Bermuda or the Azores to Lisbon, Madrid and Paris. The Constellation was sold to Iberia in February 1964 and is photographed here at Oakland on the 12th August 1963.
Lawrence Smalley via Henry Tenby (AirlineHobby.com)

LOCKHEED L-1049 SUPER CONSTELLATION

C/N4680

Delivered as a L-1049G to Qantas in November 1957 and named "Southern Zepher", this aircraft operated less than two years before being sold to Lockheed in October 1959 as N9723C. After several leases it was eventually sold to California Airmotive Corporation in May 1971, who under number 64G and named the "Red Baron", qualified at Brown Field, San Diego on 18th July 1971 to race for the US Cup but was withdrawn. The aircraft was then modified in the winter of 1971 and represented a Supersonic transport called "Condor SST" of Global Airlines in a film, and was flown by ex-Lockheed Chief Test Pilot, Herman R 'Fish' Salmon in this configuration.
Dean Slaybaugh

C/N4684

Flying over the US West Coast before delivery to the airline in early December 1957, PP-VDE displays the classic Varig livery. She was introduced on the route from Rio de Janeiro-Belém, northern Brasil-Cuidad Trujillo (now Santo Domingo), to New York in August 1955 and later with a one stop express route via Port of Spain (Trinidad) to New York. The Connies were replaced on the New York route in December 1959 with Caravelles and then Boeing 707s the following July. Super Connies also operated south on domestic services to Porto Alegre, Montevideo and Buenos Aires and later on the Sao Paulo-Rio Shuttle. The whole Constellation fleet was finally withdrawn by 1966/1967.
Lockheed - via Henry Tenby (AirlineHobby.com)

LOCKHEED L-1049 SUPER CONSTELLATION

C/N4685
Based in Rhodesia (now Zimbabwe), Afro-Continental Airways used one L-1049G Super Constellation (VP-WAW) for four years from July 1970, and operated one scheduled weekly passenger service from Salisbury (now Harare, Zimbabwe) to Windhoek in South West Africa (now Namibia), from September 1971 and general passenger and freight charters throughout South Africa. The aircraft was scrapped as late as 1990.
Peter R Keating - Scott Henderson Collection

C/N4686
Delivered new in July 1958 as "Rani of Bijapur", VT-DJW was the ninth of ten Super Constellations delivered to Air India. She was sold to No. 6 Squadron Indian Air Force as BG583 in April 1962 and, because she had been fitted with a cargo door whilst owned by Air India, was used as a long-range transport. Here she is seen at Northolt Military Airfield, London on 20th July 1962. The aircraft is currently preserved at the IAF Museum at Palam Base, Delhi.
Peter R Keating - Scott Henderson Collection

LOCKHEED L-1049 SUPER CONSTELLATION

C/N4687
VT-DJX was also eventually fitted with a cargo door by Air India and sold to the Indian Air Force as BG-579 'D' in January 1962. Here seen at Heathrow in July 1961 sporting "The Flying Sherpa" colours of Air India cargo division, the Super Conny had only five months of service left with the airline.
Brian Stainer - Scott Henderson Collection

C/N4802
At London Airport Northside, before the opening of the central terminals including the Queen's Building which would become better known as Heathrow, Seaboard & Western Airlines' L-1049H, dedicated freight Super Constellation N1006C "Prestwick Airtrader", is loaded with cargo. The aircraft was operated on scheduled cargo services between New York-Shannon-London, which was extended twice weekly to Frankfurt, with technical stops at Gander.
Brian Stainer - Scott Henderson Collection

LOCKHEED L-1049 SUPER CONSTELLATION

C/N4807
N1009C was one of two L-1049H Super Constellations leased from Seaboard World Airlines (SWA) and operated by Luxembourg based Intercontinental Airlines Inc. between May 1962 and April 1964 on passenger and freight charters across the USA. At New York in June 1963, N1009C shares the ramp with the two aircraft that were soon to replace the Constellation in service, the Boeing 707 and the Douglas DC8.
Mel Lawrence

C/N4806
Aerlinte Eireann, the predecessor to Aer Lingus, leased four L-1049 Super Constellations from April 1958 for use on the Dublin-Shannon-New York route, inaugurated on 28th April 1958. In summer it operated a daily service, but in October flights were reduced to thrice weekly, with two operating via Boston. The Connies were phased-out in late 1960 and were replaced by Boeing 720s. Here we see N1008C on lease from Seaboard & Western Airlines, newly arrived at a busy New York from Dublin in July 1959.
Mel Lawrence - Scott Henderson Collection

LOCKHEED L-1049 SUPER CONSTELLATION

C/N4808
Linea Expresa Bolivar Compania Anonima (LEBECA) owned two L-1049H Constellations. The aircraft were used on a thrice weekly freight services from Miami to Caracas, Venezuela, and also to Maracaibo, until operations ended in January 1968. YV-C-LBI sits in front of her sister aircraft YV-C-LBP whilst out of service at Miami in June 1968.
Scott Henderson Collection

C/N4810
A dramatic view of Flying Tigers' L-1049H (N6913C) climbing away from London Heathrow in June 1960, displaying the generous flap area of the Super Constellation. The aircraft was unfortunately written-off in a crash during landing at Burbank, California on the 14th December 1962.
Scott Henderson Collection

LOCKHEED L-1049 SUPER CONSTELLATION

C/N4814
At Heathrow, in early evening light, L-1049H (N6916C) awaits the next turn of duty. This aircraft
was more fortunate than N6913C and managed to pass through a succession of owners
before being broken-up at Kingman, Arizona in July 1970.
Scott Henderson Collection

C/N4815
Aéro Fletes Internacionales S.A. (AFISA) used this L-1049G, registered as HP526 "Orula", for cargo services from
Miami to Panama from August 1970 for two years until 1972 when the company lost its permit to fly
and the aircraft was grounded.
Scott Henderson Collection

LOCKHEED L-1049 SUPER CONSTELLATION

C/N4816
Nasantara Airways of Jakarta was issued a licence to operate domestic and international flights for the Indonesian Government. They leased N6916C from Flying Tigers, with eight more assigned, but unfortunately this aircraft was impounded during the delivery flight in Singapore on 21st September 1968, and not released until May 1969 only to be impounded again at Hong Kong. It was released in June and returned to the airline, but was destined never to operate any services for NAL.
TAHS

C/N4818
A rather interesting shot of N101R, a L-1049H, taken during a two year lease from the Dynalectron Corporation of Washington. Mel Lawrence does the honours and records the occasion at Tachikawa, Japan in September 1961.
Mel Lawrence

LOCKHEED L-1049 SUPER CONSTELLATION

C/N4819
Seen on a miserable day at Osaka, Japan, L-1049H Super Constellation HL 4002 of Korean Airlines makes a rare sight as it is serviced for flight, seven months into its twelve month lease from Flying Tiger Line.
Mel Lawrence - Scott Henderson Collection

C/N4820
In early 1961, World Airways Inc. of Oakland leased five L-1049H Constellations to service its recently gained 'MATS' passenger/cargo contracts to Manila, Tokyo, Okinawa and Bangkok, and also domestic services. The airline eventually used a total of eleven Constellations of different marks within its fleet before the withdrawal of the type in 1964 to be replaced by Boeing 707s. At Oakland in February 1962, N1880 sits idle with interesting company.
Mel Lawrence - Scott Henderson Collection

LOCKHEED L-1049 SUPER CONSTELLATION

C/N4820
N1880 was leased to Transocean from the 1880 Corporation, for a period of twenty-one months from 9th July 1957 to March 1959, for use on the airline's low fare routes from Oakland and Burbank, California to Honolulu, Hawaii.
TAHS

C/N4821
Peter Keating took this interesting shot at St Hubert, Canada of Hellenic Air Ltd. L-1049 (CF-AEN) on 1st August 1972. A former Transocean and Capital International Airways aircraft, the Connie was sold to Canairelief Air in November 1969 and used on the Biafran Airlift until return to Canada in 1970 for sale to Hellenic Air. However the sale was cancelled and the aircraft languished at St Herbert, Montreal, until it was finally broken up in June 1974.
Peter R Keating

LOCKHEED L-1049 SUPER CONSTELLATION

C/N4829
Former National Airlines' N7132C, now re-registered as CF-NAK with the small Canadian airline Nordair,
is loaded with cargo at Dorval, Canada in October 1967. The aircraft was destroyed in a bombing
raid at Uli airstrip, Biafra (Nigeria) on 17th December 1969 whilst operated and owned
by Canairelief Air Ltd.
Peter R Keating - Scott Henderson Collection

C/N4830
In June 1966, Airlift took over the assets of Slick Airways, acquiring the bankrupt airline's fleet of L-1049H
Constellations. All the aircraft were used for US Military Airlift Command (MAC) charters from the
company's Miami base until the last aircraft was retired and replaced by DC8s in late 1967.
Scott Henderson Collection

LOCKHEED L-1049 SUPER CONSTELLATION

C/N4831

N7133C of National Airlines of Miami displays its colourful "Airline of the Stars" livery while on a test flight from Long Beach, prior to delivery to the airline in October 1957.
Lockheed

C/N4831

The first organisation to restore a Super Constellation to flying condition was Kanas City based "Save-a-Connie", a group of former TWA employees who rescued and restored L-1049H (N6937C) to her former glory carrying the colours but not the full livery of TWA. Since the demise of the Airline, the aircraft has been restored to the full livery of Trans World Airlines, which she carries on the US air show circuit.
Scott Henderson

LOCKHEED L-1049 SUPER CONSTELLATION

C/N4832
Ex-Nordair L-1049H (CF-NAM) is seen on 4th May 1969 at Dorval Airport, Montreal, awaiting delivery to Canairelief
Air. After relief service during the Biafran war in Nigeria when the aircraft received bomb damage
at Uli Airport, she was withdrawn from use and flown to São Tomé, an island 200 miles off the
coast of Gabon, to be stored. It is believed she still exists in derelict condition.
Peter R Keating - Scott Henderson Collection

C/N4834
Arguably wearing the most beautiful livery to grace the Constellation in service, PP-YSB was the second of four L-1049H
Super Constellations bought in March 1958 by Redes Estaduais Aéreas Limitida (REAL S.A.) of Sao Paulo, Brazil.
They were operated on the Buenos Aires-Montevideo-Sao Paulo-Rio-Port of Spain-Miami route, and also the
Sao Paulo-Rio-Caracas-Miami route. In 1960 the service from Mexico City to Los Angeles was added, and
this was later extended to Hawaii, Wake Island and Tokyo. In between May and August 1961, Varig took
control of the airline and incorporated the Super Constellations into their fleet.
Peter R Keating - Scott Henderson Collection

LOCKHEED L-1049 SUPER CONSTELLATION

C/N4834

At New York in July 1963, PP-YSB displays the change of livery undertaken when REAL was merged with Varig in 1961.
Mel Lawrence

C/N4836

The last of five Lockheed L-1049H Super Constellations for Pakistan Airlines, AP-AJZ passes through London Airport
Northside during her delivery flight to Karachi on 5th March 1958. The aircraft was operated on domestic services
from Karachi-Lahore (West Pakistan) to Dacca (East Pakistan), and on the international service
Karachi-Barrhain-Rome/Genéva-London. Withdrawn in 1969, the aircraft
was donated with two others to the Indonesian Air Force.
Brian Stainer - Scott Henderson Collection

LOCKHEED L-1049 SUPER CONSTELLATION

C/N4843
Delivered new to KLM as "Hermannus Boerhaave" on 14th May 1958, this was the last Super Constellation delivered to the airline. It operated tourist flights to North America until the end of the year, when it was converted to all-cargo configuration for scheduled Amsterdam-Montreal-New York and Amsterdam-Curaao- (West Dutch Indies)-New York services. Here we see PH-LKN taking a well earned rest after flying half-way across the world from Amsterdam to Tokyo in May 1961.
Mel Lawrence - Scott Henderson Collection

C/N4843
N45515 of KLM Royal Dutch Airlines is photographed in between flights at Chicago, Ohare in June 1964, wearing the liveries of both World Airways (who had leased the aircraft for twelve months from July 1962) and Flying Tiger Line who further leased N45515 from August 1963. The Connie was eventually bought by the airline in May 1966.
Mel Lawrence

LOCKHEED L-1049 SUPER CONSTELLATION

C/N4847

Aerolessors Inc. of Miami began cargo operations in 1966 to the Caribbean and Central and South America with this Super Constellation, with two more arriving in 1967 and 1968. N469C was operated on regular arms flights for two months from Lisbon to Fernando Po, Uli Biafra beginning September 1968. Pictured at Sebring, Florida five months before being withdrawn from service. She was eventually broken up in 1980, whilst the airline stopped trading in 1970.
Harry Sievers - Peter R Keating

C/4847

Air Mid East, with offices at Syracuse, New York and in the Middle East at Athens and Beirut, used one L-1049H for less than one month. Carrying this livery she arrived at Madrid in mid July 1968 and picked up a cargo for Biafra, and then flew on to Fernando Po and awaited permission to fly into Uli, Biafra. However the Biafran authorities refused permission, and the Connie was forced to return to the USA.
TAHS

LOCKHEED L-1049 SUPER CONSTELLATION

C/N4849
Originally delivered new to Slick Airways Inc. in September 1959, Mel Lawrence has caught N6936C in a quiet moment
at Tachikawa, Japan in April 1960. After a merger with Airlift International in July 1966, the aircraft
was lost in a mid-air collision with an RF-4C Phantom near Saigon,
South Vietnam on 22nd June 1967.
Mel Lawrence - Scott Henderson Collection

C/N4850
The sole L-1049H in the fleet of Central American Airways, N74CA was purchased from Necal Aircraft Leasing in
January 1973 and spent most of its life transporting automobile parts around the USA. The aircraft
was written-off in a crash during take-off at Columbus, Ohio in June 1980
whilst flying for Air Traders International.
Scott Henderson Collection

LOCKHEED L-1049 SUPER CONSTELLATION

C/N4853

After two lease periods, Trans International Airlines purchased N6925C, a L-1049H from Tracy Lease and Finance Corporation in March 1964 and used the aircraft on freight charters and military contracts from its Los Angeles base for two years six months until onward sale to Flying Tiger Lines. Here we see the aircraft on the ramp at Gatwick in April 1965.
Scott Henderson Collection

C/N5506

"Paisano" Bu145925 was delivered to the US Navy on 28th January 1958 as a WV-2, and served with Airborne Early Warning Squadrons VW-1 and VW-3 at Adana Guam until 1961, when it was stored at Litchfiels Park, Arizona. After the crash of 126513 "El Paisano" in October 1960 at McMurdo Sound in the Antarctic, its dedicated equipment was removed and fitted to 145925 by LAS to become "El Paisano Dos (2)" a specially modified EC-121K with an airborne magnetomer, used to check variations in the earth's magnetic field for 'Project Magnet'. The aircraft was operated in this guise until May 1973, when replaced by a Lockheed Orion.
Scott Henderson Collection

LOCKHEED L-1649 STARLINER

C/N1002
World Samplers, a travel club organisation, leased N7301C from Charles E Bush Aviation, from August 1965 for
International Charters for club members. On one of these trips to Mexico City on 13th August 1965,
the Starliner is seen boarding passengers in preparation for the return flight to the USA.
Leon Franco - Henry Tenby (AirlineHobby.com)

C/N1003
The Flying Ambassadors Travel Club also leased L-1649 (N7302C) from Charles E Bush Aviation, for travel charters for
club members from February 1966. Once again at Mexico City in March 1966, the aircraft patiently awaits
the return of club passengers for the return flight to the United States.
Leon Franco - Henry Tenby (AirlineHobby.com)

LOCKHEED L-1649 STARLINER

C/N1006
Trans Atlantica Argentina purchased four L-1640 Starliners including LV-GLH, from Trans World Airlines of the US for international services from Buenos Aires to London and Geneva via Rio de Janeiro and Lisbon. However the airline found trading conditions hard considering that the competition was mostly flying jet aircraft, and this caused the airline to suspend all operations in November 1961.
Brian Stainer - Scott Henderson Collection

C/N1011
Air France L-1649A (F-BHBK), one of ten Starliners used by the airline, demonstrates the increased wing area which enabled the Lockheed designers to move the engines a further five feet out from the fuselage. This was a popular feature with the passengers as it reduced the drone of the piston engines in the cabin.
Lockheed - Henry Tenby (AirlineHobby.com)

LOCKHEED L-1649 STARLINER

C/N1016
The classic lines of TWA Starliner N7314C "Jetstream, Star of the Shannon" grace the ramp at Heathrow Airport in April 1962. The airline was the major user of the L-1649, having taken delivery of 25 new and also purchasing four on the second-hand market.
Peter R Keating - Scott Henderson Collection

C/N1018
Now withdrawn from service and preserved at Auburn-Lewiston Airport, Maine, N7316C starts engines in preparation for flight whilst in service with Alaska Airlines. The airline operated a total of six Starliners between 1962 until 1968, for both freight and passenger service in the US and also for "MATS" flights to Europe.
Nicky Scherrer

LOCKHEED L-1649 STARLINER

C/N 1025

In May 1968, Aerovias Halcon of Argentina leased N7322C, now converted into a freighter, from California Airmotive Corporation for a six month period in May 1968, for the transportation of horses and cattle. In this shot of the aircraft during a visit to Mexico City in November 1968, loading is about to begin.
Leon Franco - Henry Tenby (AirlineHobby.com)

C/N 1026

Willair International leased one L-1649 (N8081H) from California Airmotive Corporation in April 1968 for use in transporting cattle-hide from Spain to Taiwan for the manufacture of leather goods and then to return the finished goods back to the USA. Unfortunately the aircraft was badly damaged at Stockton, California on 10th June 1968 when the undercarriage collapsed, as can be seen in this photograph, and the aircraft was scrapped soon after.
Henry Tenby - Scott Henderson Collection

LOCKHEED L-1649 STARLINER

C/N1031
Air Afrique leased F-BHBO of Air France for its African services in partial Air France colours and re-registered the aircraft as TU-TBA for a period of twenty months from October 1961. On return from the lease, the aircraft was stored at Paris-Orly until it was broken up in August 1967.
Scott Henderson Collection

C/N1036
Ex-Trek Airways, LX-LGY, was flown by little known "Nittler Air Transport" for a period of two and a half years during which time freight services were flown from the US to Panama with the aircraft re-registered HP-501. Eventually the Starliner found its way to Douala in the Cameroon, Central West Africa, where it was eventually scrapped in 1980.
Scott Henderson Collection

LOCKHEED L-1649 STARLINER

C/N1040
N179AV sits idle on the Gatwick ramp during a charter to the UK. She was owned by Air Venturers, a US Travel Club based in Houston Texas, who purchased the Starliner in March 1966 for International Charters. Unlike most other L-1649A aircraft, N179AV was destined to survive being scrapped and for two decades languished at Sanford Florida awaiting her fate. She was later ferried to the Kermit Weeks Fantasy of Flight Museum, Florida for preservation, wearing the Lufthansa colours that she wore when brand new.
Scott Henderson Collection

C/N1041
One of four Starliners purchased new by Lufthansa, D-ALER delivered to the airline in January 1958, displays her lines during a service flight to New York. After five years with Trek Airways of South Africa, the aircraft was withdrawn from service in 1969 and after less than a year in storage, was broken up in May 1970.
Lufthansa

LOCKHEED L-1649 STARLINER

CC/N1042
ZS-DVJ of Trek Airways displays her colourful livery at Johannesburg on 18th May 1969. Previously owned by Lufthansa, she was bought by Trek in February 1964 for services to Europe in co-operation with Luxair of Luxembourg. In 1969 the aircraft was withdrawn from service and today is fully restored as the centre-piece of the South African Airways collection at Johannesburg.
Peter R Keating - Scott Henderson Collection

C/N1042
Leased for a period of one year in May 1967 from Trek Airways, ZS-DVJ was re-registered as LX-LGX and flown in association with Trek on European services wearing the full colours of Luxair. Peter R Keating took this photograph of the Starliner at London Gatwick on 21st August 1967 during a rare idle period.
Peter R Keating - Scott Henderson Collection

INDEX OF AIRLINES

SCOVAL
PUBLISHING LTD